RAGTIME IN UNFAMILIAR BARS

RON BUTLIN

Ragtime in Unfamiliar Bars

SECKER & WARBURG
LONDON

First published in England 1985 by
Martin Secker & Warburg Limited
54 Poland Street, London W1V 3DF

Copyright © Ron Butlin 1985

British Library Cataloguing in Publication Data

Butlin, Ron
  Ragtime in unfamiliar bars.
  I. Title
  821'.914   PR6052.U8/

  ISBN 0–436–07810–4

Typeset by Inforum Ltd, Portsmouth
Printed in England by
Redwood Burn Ltd, Trowbridge

To Roger

ACKNOWLEDGEMENTS

Some of these poems have appeared previously in *AFM*, *The Antigonish Review*, *Bananas*, *Cencrastus*, *Creatures Tamed by Cruelty* (Edinburgh University SPB), *Descant* (Toronto), *Encounter*, *The Green River Review*, *Lines Review*, *Lot 49*, *National Book League Writers in Brief No 19*, *New Edinburgh Review*, *New Statesman*, *Paris/Atlantic*, *The Poetry Book Society Christmas Supplement*, *The Poetry of Motion*, *Poetry Review*, *Quarto*, *The Scotsman*, *The Times Literary Supplement*, *La Traductière*, *Radio Scotland*, *Radio 3*.

'This Embroidery' is reprinted from *The Exquisite Instrument* published by The Salamander Press.

I would like to thank the Scottish Arts Council, University of Edinburgh, University of New Brunswick, Canada Council and Deans Community High School who have allowed me time to complete this book.

CONTENTS

RAGTIME IN UNFAMILIAR BARS

ST CLOUD IN THE SPRING

Of the many versions of spring this one is mine
for the present: a suddenly coloured-in garden
beneath an imperfect blue sky where inaccurate
songbirds keep changing their tune
as they fly round the sun. I lie and I wait
for my past to catch up – and it doesn't. I integrate
nothing and nothing's omitted, and nothing's to come
– not the droughts of November nor the snowfalls in June.

DESCRIPTIONS OF THE FALLING SNOW

I described a flight of imaginary birds
across an imaginary sky in words
that played out every laboured game of skill
involving consonants and vowels, until
sufficient universal truths obeyed
the cadences of my trade.

I argued love and metaphysics through
by sound, resolving dissonance into
a line of formal spontaneity:
a passionate description of, let's say,
the falling snow. These were not dreams
but calculations for what seems

a well-constructed winter sky. Neatly
stammered syllables of discreetly
quantified despair described the view:
some fields of hardened grass and mud; a few
abandoned tractors; a waterfall's cascade
stiffening into ice. I made

events from over twenty years ago
translate into each metaphor – as though
a door slammed shut, or someone's name
had set the limits to my suffering.
(And if the phrase read awkwardly I'd pause,
checking each effect for flaws.)

The qualities of light through falling snow;
the patterns made by frost; the fields below
my house – I scanned and stressed a thousand words
describing everything I saw. The birds
in flight across the imaginary skies
sang what I set down – my lies

were coming true. And yet, I cannot live
uncorrupted by the narrative
I tell. All things are mine to name:
there is no innocence, no shame;
nothing is, that is not of my own
and of my incantation.

My fingers claw at imaginary birds.
My tongue stutters over lists of words
I've learnt by heart. Such passionate pretence!
It is almost five o'clock. I sense
the hammer strike the bell and cancel-out
each pitiless belief and doubt.

AT BOULOGNE

It was almost raining when we met.
I remember concrete customs sheds, low cloud, wet
timber, a chilling sea-wind, a stack
of rusting tins and some black
grit heaped against a padlocked door.
Onto the watered-down shore
wash oiled sea-colours; the sky leaks
its weakest pigments, leaving streaks
the wind gathers and smears
across two frontiers.
A damp patch does for a horizon
where nothing is happening.

'The hovercraft seems rather late.'
Silence. I watch the sea evaporate
slowly while several feet away
you ignore my opening remark. Its spontaneity
was well prepared. – In lieu
of further preparation I repeat myself.
And so do you.

The November sun slides slowly upwards through
a greasy haze. A minute passes. Two
minutes pass. If it was still divine I'd pray
– but melting minerals and inert gases pay
such little heed to me. My mortal recipe
(two parts benevolence to three parts greed)
makes God, whether argued *a priori*
or seen in three instalments, less a certainty
than a Devil cloned to individual need.
For, with former dead, the latter's taken heed
the latter's taken heed
and modernised: no messy blood-and-parchment now
but hi-tech psycho-system software. A silent vow,
computerised, will instantly allow

each man to choose his own temptation-terms. The old
Mephisto middle-men are out – damnation is controlled
directly by the sinner. No fuss, no queues, no pain.
Five million souls a second – and no last minute slips
of conscience . . . I hear what might be silicon chips
rattling in hell . . . All's well. I've sold
myself for just the right amount of rain
required to start a conversation.

   I glance in your direction, smile then casually unfold
my umbrella. I begin, 'Perhaps you'd care
to share my –' then stop right there.
Something's wrong. The air is growing warmer!
The devil, perhaps confused by former
dealings – or thinking the bargain's bad – transmutes
the leaden clouds to gold.

   My pea-green jacket with brown boots,
checkered shirt and flannels have already told
all Europe where I'm from. But one moment's folly
has sometimes made our nation great:
I remark upon the change in weather, then hesitate
no longer but open out my British Brolly
to give, to both of us at once, complete
protection from the sudden Continental Heat.

PICCADILLY: A FINAL ENTERTAINMENT

Not wishing to sleep in the streets I've built a palace
invisible to passers-by. It stretches from here
to here; it's made of white-noise, a glance
and uncertainty.

The statue of a young god stands in the centre. A handclasp,
a half-smile, a casual remark:
– and boy-priests are smeared with his divinity.

This is the high-life: where goddesses claim me; where sunlight
discolours the skin stretched tight across lips,
wrists and skulls; where the dying
preach immortality.

As a final entertainment I shall conjure darkness
to be lit by my familiars.
Together we shall enter paradise as ghosts:
as a final entertainment we shoot to kill.

RESTORATION OF A PAINTED CITY

The Clouds

The clouds were still drifting above Canaletto's Venice
when winter came.

They drifted into calculated sunlight
where they were coloured in.

They were photographed and made secure.

Our Room

The paintwork was so bare and badly cracked
we watched sunlight and moonlight
come shining through the walls.

When winter came our window was replaced
by a stroke of black paint.

The Acts of Restoration

The affairs of men and women are restored
to what they were two hundred years ago.

The Grand Canal and quayside are scraped
of two centuries' sea-fog and grime.

She sits at the mirror
making certain each smear of make-up
is perfectly in place.

She says she must return home.
She tugs hard at strands of hair
– her eyes filling with tears.

The City of Venice

Helplessly I list the possibilities:

That she will accompany the Doge's retinue;
That sunlight and moonlight will come shining through
our open window;

That the perfume she is wearing lingers
for two hundred years; That her fingers
rest lightly on the kinsman's arm
whose skill at playing courtier will charm
even with its silence, the silent Doge;

That those few moments' artistry with rouge
and lipstick will deceive two centuries' decay
– until one kiss creates another possibility.

ORPHEUS GIVES AN ENCORE

When they awake it is midwinter: a London bedsit.,
floral curtains, iced-up windows – and for
the roaring surf at Delphos there's the hiss
of faulty central heating.
Next-door, a closet Monteverdi howls aloud
his breakfast madrigals and canzonette
in as many parts as he can manage
while his kettle boils
drier than any *secco* recitative.

The Hero's triumph over death is symbolised
by simple gestures, stretching and the like,
performed with caution lest his touch suggest
awakening desire.
The Heroine lies still. She remembers nothing
of the songs that charmed her here last night,
only the rain upon a corrugated-
iron roof, hammering
out applause after the final chorus.

They kiss awkwardly and feel obliged to give
an encore. There's the hiss of Stygian waters
and, on cue, the gondolier next-door
begins to sound like Charon.
Terrified they'll lose one moment's tenderness,
her ghost and his mortality embrace.
Winter sunlight chills the room and lays
discoloured flowers, shuddering
at the slightest draught, upon them both.

ARGENTINA 1978

A ship lies gasping in the cupboard:
its crew disturbs my sleep night after night
with their demands to put to sea.

– But no soone- do I close my eyes
and start imagining to myself the long ball
from Bruce Rioch that I take past one man, side-
flick past a second and am lining up for a Peter Lorimer-
rocket-postage-stamp in the top right-hand corner
while the crowd goes wild, wild, wild
– when from behind the terraces I hear the opening strains
of the first of that evening's many sea-shanties.

I try to ignore it, and tell myself that back home
all Scotland's sitting boozed and bunneted in front of the TV,
watching me with only the goalie to beat
and the World Cup as good as on the mantelpiece.

– But already the crowd's been infiltrated;
already some of them
(I suspect the ones with eye-patches,
and anchors over their shoulders)
have started singing 'Hearts of Oak'
in counterpoint to the crowd's roar
– and I see the goal-posts and netting sway gently
in an easterly breeze.

I try to ignore it for the ball's still at my feet
and I tell myself that back home
all Scotland's standing on the sofas and the sideboards
cheering themselves tartan.

– But already the Easterly has freshened up,
the goal-posts are listing slightly
and, as the netting billows, are pulling away from the terraces
where *everyone*'s now wearing an eye-patch
and has an anchor over his shoulder
– some of them are even watching the game through telescopes!
10

I try to ignore them and line up the ball for the big one,
the one that's going to be the one and only,
the most beautiful thing to come out of Scotland
since McEwan's Export,
the one they'll action-replay till the film falls apart.

The crowd gives out with 'Steady boys, steady!'
I try to ignore it
– the ball turns into a pink bobbing marker-buoy!
I try to ignore it
– the goals are towing the terraces of shantying sailors

                                               out to sea!
I try to ignore it:
Scotland's not going to be robbed, not this time!

Then suddenly I am alone in Argentina.
No crowd, no ball, no goals, no cup.
The grass is turning to sea-water
– and it's a long swim home!

IN A JAPANESE GIRL'S ROOM

You guided me through opium
while walking high above the streets of Tokyo.

You said, 'Let's enter this deserted building
and climb these stairs to the roof,
if no one's watching let's kiss.
Though it's too cold to undress
and too wet to lie down
let's make the best of it while we can.'

Then you said you would perform the tea-ceremony
as you had done for thousands of years;
and afterwards we undressed by candlelight,
and afterwards we lay in tears.

THIS EMBROIDERY

I have laid your clothes out on our bed;
smoothing the lace, the silk and satin finery
seam by seam.

Only a mess of coloured thread
remains to fold away;
this embroidery you said was part-dream
and part-imaginary.

You would have finished it next spring.
These chalk-marks are clouds, and these – men fishing.

BEFORE LEAVING

Do you remember who made love an hour ago?
They lived for too short a time – and so

before leaving I will pull you close:
your lips will press on mine
reprieving a lifetime, even
for the length of a kiss.

THIS EVENING

You placed yellow roses by the window, then,
leaning forwards, began combing your red hair;
perhaps you were crying.
To make the distance less I turned away
and faced you across the earth's circumference.

The window-pane turns black:
across its flawed glass suddenly your image
runs on mine.
I stare at the vase until yellow
is no longer a colour, nor the roses flowers.

INDIAN SUMMER

As though time passes. Drenched in silver
and pale gold an ocean seems to break
beneath us; it brings together night
and day imperfectly.

As though each sliding contour of the sky
has paused, the colours of the clouds
saturate the ocean.

As though it is a late September afternoon
we sit drinking wine outdoors;
the dusklight falls between our hands
and soaks into the grass.

Soon, moonlight will stain the ocean-floor:
sea-creatures will take fright
and turn away.

NIGHT-LIFE

My nerves are stretched tight above the city:
a night-map of neon and sodium.

Hours earlier you wore darkness as love itself:
moonlight you ground more finely with each kiss,
starlight you scattered out of reach.

And now, what burning inside me?
what light trapped in a clenched sky?

THE PHILOSOPHER TURNS ACCOUNTANT

I've listened long enough to those who state:
'Love needs no past or future; only *this*
is real; retrospective thoughts translate
but poorly into philosophic bliss;
that having kissed, the truly wise will let
the kisses go . . .' Their logic's fine, their premise
only I dispute, for none has met
or ever been in love with you
                              – or else he too
would free himself from wisdom, and growing yet
more wise, forget his theories, reminisce
most shamelessly as now I'm forced to do.

I live on your account, cross-tabulate
each item thus: your voice, your hair, your face
when smiling, perfume, touch. I calculate
your presence with these sad inventories,
converting their precious currency for private
circulation. Your absence is the base-rate.
I dream, imagine, appropriate
and hoard all such brief epiphanies.
        My miserly affection will,
with love and metaphysical disgrace,
guide me well enough until
we can more cost-effectively embrace.

THE NIGHT-SKY, THE RIVER AND THE
SCENT OF SYCAMORE

While we talked long-distance the night-sky entered my room
and the St John river became a thick black line
drawn through trees and streetlights
– these were the elements of your voice.

Afterwards I stared at the parking-lot outside
while forcing the clock's hands months beyond
half-shut curtains, a print of Lake Niagara,
strip-lighting and an unmade bed.

I know these things are the clumsy antecedents of nothing
yet your absence is all around me; and your nakedness,
the scent of sycamore carried on the night-air.

MOZART'S LAST YEAR

I picture him one summer's evening:
it's warm, he's seated by an open window
writing to Michael Puchberg. He's thirty
-five years old: no longer that most charming
music-box they'd praised and passed from hand
to hand in all the courts of Europe – for when
his tunes began to sound ever so slightly
déjà vu, they threw him out.

He's writing from the suburbs of Vienna, begging
for money. At night he dreams of Papageno:
he hears the bird-catcher's song while lime is shovelled
upon his upturned face.

ABOVE SAANAN

If this were a dark country lit only by fragments of the sun,
a mountainside the colour of its flowers, how many colours
would I need were I describing this, above Saanan
– above its roofs, its streets and trees, its single-track railway?

If someone's hand pressed hard against my eyes, their voice
                                                        demanding
'Guess who?' – whose name would I cry aloud while clutching
at the sound of running water, the cicada's noise
or at a glider's silence passing overhead?

I watch as pastureland and forest-colours dark-green, red
and gold, establish early autumn. This, above Saanan,
is flower-light now, spread across a darkened country,
and an empty sky suddenly stained blue.

THE KINGDOM BUILT ON WATER

There is a kingdom built on water
where insects glide haphazardly
among the clouds and the blue buildings of the priests.

At other times it is a night-sky reversed
and held motionless, or a cloudless day
when the curving roofs and battlements are traced

and then retraced by a lapwing passing overhead.

*

There is a king who is both male and female;
there are painted animals
and evenings among women and young boys.

Both sexes struggle within him: blackness
run through with silver;
sunlight obscured by rain.

Silence is matched by silence.

*

Astrologers catalogue the heavens' disarray;
architects plan palaces and pleasure-gardens,
slaves build them and die.
The king looks on.

Perfection spreads carelessly from one moment
to the next, holding him fast.
The clouds and the blue buildings of the priests slide
effortlessly out of reach.

22

Having traced the histories of how men love
and how they cease to love,
the king sets painted animals to hunt
his women and young boys

– sometimes letting them go, or silencing them
with a kiss.

*

For thirty years I have gazed upon a kingdom built on water.

Whatever I have seen I have seen perish, excepting this:

a woman's image rising from the bottom of the lake,
she reaches for me as though drowning
when I take her in my arms.

She is rain piercing the stonework of the palace,
moonlight glazing my eyes with silver:

She is everything ruined and precious.

TWO PLAYERS

Two players who have made-up so often
their faces seem to shine with love,
approach each other in the palace gardens.
Something has been arranged. Orpheus
begins to charm his way once more
with a clear conscience and a song.
Eurydice trails behind

stumbling among the props and deafening
effects – the stones, the wheels, the hiss
of accusation and desire.
Orpheus makes his way towards the wings
without a backward glance.
He sings of love, truth and beauty.

Though the palace is only three months old
Eurydice feels its pillars buckling at a touch;
she sees the tiled floor crack at each step
and the colours drain away.
Off-stage peacocks scream, or seem to.

She has nothing to say. With each lighting-change
a host of shadows lunge
and swoop around her, parodying large
her exquisite and mute anxieties.

Until the very last moment Orpheus acts
without hesitation, and he mimes perfectly
whatever he leaves unsung.

The shadows slide into each other voluptuously:
which of these lovers will lead him out of Hell?

He turns to kiss Eurydice goodbye.

FELLOW-TRAVELLERS

Where timbrel, gong and drone sound invisibly;
where colours come only to those cuts of fruit
I dip into the spring and then to the patches of hard bark,
sand and the few slender stems I splash
in raising the fruit to my lips – there I drink deeply.

As the morning's heat sets the desert contours vibrating
so I – the more slow, the more dull with each mouthful of
                                        clear water –
see between the several moments of the day, between
the certainties of hunger and thirst, slopes of soft sand
stretching to the distance. – And between them,

between the shifting grains which a single breath of wind
could cause to cut me to the heart and make
my eyes weep, I see a fellow-traveller approach;
drawn, perhaps by the sound of unseen musicians
or the promise of water and fruit, to the same mirage.

LETTING GO

No longer a green orchard, nor blue;
for my hands are letting go
– even as you glance in my direction
my hands let go their jewels.

No longer an orchard nor the ocean
we saw surrounding us
– for even the taste of salt and grit are the same,
like sea-spray and precious stones.

ONCE UPON A TIME

The banisters slide up through the rain.
She cannot hold on – her body slips backwards
into the waterfall.

We struggle upstairs separately
towards a broken skylight, a single-bar fire
and damp sheets.

Once upon a time I carried her all the way to the top.
Now she clutches at falling water
to pull herself up.

TWO WOMEN

The room is stacked high with caged birds.
Feathers cover the floor.
One woman brings out tequila
while another, almost a child,
brings lemon, salt and a small sharp knife.

The old woman's songs are slovenly,
she makes herself cry. Then,
kicking up feathers, she makes the child dance through down-
drifting scarlet, vermilion and gold:
desert-colours for her lips, her breasts and her thighs;
the deadness of desert-light in her eyes.

PREPARATIONS FOR A SEA-VOYAGE

It was like this: we made the spare oars
from wax; the ropes from weed;
smoke we gathered into sails, and the prow
was once the concentration of a cat.

After the embarkation party the doors
and hatches were slammed shut and screw-locked
– yet gatecrashers and their girls, their relatives
and their girls somehow barged in,
promising to row.
We knew they never would. Instead
we forced them onto all-fours
to scrub the decks, the cannons, the cannon-balls,
the cabin-floors and holds.
We gave them mops, pails and promises of rum,
then left them.

In time they finished off their chores.
They caught and scraped sea-creatures clean
of phosphorescence.
(How the decks will shine at night!)
The mast, cut from the shortest distance
between two points sixty feet apart they carved
and then inlaid with sea-tusk ivory
and oyster-shell.
New arrangements of shanties, jigs and reels
were made and photocopied for the crew;
they macraméd all the tangled ropes then neatly
lettered each one through like rock,
'in memoriam all those lost at sea
since Salamis'.
We expressed our thanks, suggested
they might form a chamber orchestra
or leave. They left.

When our automatic pilot tracked down
the setting sun we cut the anchor free
and opened more champagne.
And now – full speed ahead!
I fear these oars and sails will not remain
as oars and sails for very long.

ELEGY

You are lying in my arms more loved by me
than any woman I have ever known,
and yet the fear of losing you has proved to be
my love's undoing. Each caress has shown
another source for our despair:
we touch and share a sense of certain loss to come;
we snatch at time as at each colour
sunlight spills into your room.
Because we die each moment let us love the more,
and let love's metaphor be *resurrection*.

A GENTLE DEMOLITION

Let us summon what real love there was
and free it now, before it is too late.
No conditions. Our rules and very private
statutes need repeal as every clause
at once turns advocate to plead the cause
of separation – urging us to hate
and so survive. We cannot legislate
and love, nor barter promises as laws.
And so, before we're forced to play the prison-
scenes of our particular despair,
that precedents and repetitious passion
will in time condemn us to, let's tear
this court-house down – a gentle demolition;
then leave as friends or lawyers might – together.

AT THE PIANO

The numbers, the colours and names that lay
in your hand were a song you soundlessly played
above hammers, levers and strings.

Your fingers were pressing down keys; they released
as silence spanning one moment, the naming,
the counting and colouring-in

of all that you were, so briefly, just then.
What are the confusions of love, time
and despair – set against this?

AN ITALIAN LANDSCAPE

Where rain is wearing the stones down.
Where flowers and frosts split the stones.

I hear wings beating against our bedroom window . . .

We shall gather flowers perfect in every detail
and fragments of mineral and bone.

Then we shall piece everything together:

trees, vineyards, sunlight, some fields
and in the distance a lake, perhaps.

. . . trapped in the slowly breaking glass.

BELIEVE ME

Go to the first-floor of a boarding-house
in Acton High St London,
and from 6pm each evening you will find
a man who has no friends.

He listens to radio stations that are further
and further away. He will show you
charts he has made and textbooks
he has read. His wife lives upstairs.

With the sound down he aligns the aerial
so perfectly you recognise 'Top Hat'
sung in Swahili.

Then, when insistent and out of time foot-, cane-
and furniture-stamping begins upstairs,
he will produce two sets of headphones and,
believe me, it is time to leave.

THE EMBROIDERESS

I watch her fingers busily stitch men
and women upon a roll of cloth.
I watch as they embrace in silence,
then slowly tear themselves apart.

For a moment she glances from her work
and beckons me towards her.
Her flesh and bone I breathe into myself;
her spirit settles on my lips and eyes.

Fascinated I watch my fingers work busily
leaving a trail of men and women
upon a roll of cloth.

For too long I have been struggling with this dream
of endless stitching and endless mutilation:
everything depends upon the moment of awakening
– a moment that may have already passed.

RAGTIME IN UNFAMILIAR BARS

I'm teaching Peter how to play a suite
in the style of J.S. Bach complete
with grace-notes. He suspects I improvise
the rules myself; I sit back, close my eyes
and bid him conscientiously repeat
each dreary trill. This exercise

can kill at least ten minutes. 'To modulate:
all keys and accidentals should relate
in your imagination *before* you play,
so take your time.' He's bored and doesn't pay
attention – yet, he nods. 'Deliberate –'
He yawns. '–letting silence weigh

out sound as theme and counter-theme. Don't run
at it.' He shakes his head. I feel done-in.
Eleven minutes more and our release
will come; meanwhile, another masterpiece
to get through! The central heating's turned full on
I'm almost fast asleep. Grease

from Peter's lunchtime toast and tea covers
his fingers; keys stick; the score wavers
in the heat as bar-lines and breves macramé
tilting treble-clefs to weave in swami-
contemplations of their staves; quavers
are held fast in origami

tangles of tied-notes. My voice drones on.
Beyond the triple-glazing a winter sun
shines white, without heat, on snow. As if
to hear more clearly garden plants stand stiff,
stripped down to their stalks and at attention,
antennaed for the slightest whiff

of J.S.B. – the perfect audience:
well-cultivated and without pretence!
Peter's too-abruptly phrased allegro
counterpoints my dull, tireless flow
of index-linked advice: 'and *four* . . . and sense
the beat . . . and *one* and *two* . . . and know

not only *when* – your metronome will show
. . . and *three* . . . but *how* . . . Play each arpeggio
to modulate these weeks of diligence
into one moment's grace.' The dissonance
of *his* despair fits neatly in a row
of minor thirds. Adolescence

celebrates delicious and very private
harmonies – not music, but intimate
sweet nothings told only to soothe the pain.
– And later, a composer? – A teaching-machine:
'Left-hand, right-hand, both together'. I hate
when they demand 'an easy nocturne',

– premeditated massacres, complete
with sighs, long silences and both their feet
upon the pedals! We sit like father and son?
– master and man more like! A buttered scone,
a cup of milky Earl Grey, discreet
I-won't-disturb-you smiles; this vision

of maternal tact then drifts next door
to strain the leaves again before she'll pour
more water in the pot. Double cream,
jam and powdered coconut redeem
her afternoon. Last week she asked: 'I'm sure
Peter's coming on a *dream* . . .

Has he begun on Brahms? Bach can be
so very dull at twelve, I'd hate to see
him bored. One doesn't like to interfere,
of course, but *Brahms*!' An hour's walk from here
my 'Oratorio Profane' for three
hundred voices, children's choir

and pre-recorded tape rots in piles
upon the floor. De-structured parables
inter-cut Ecclesiastes; the last
words of Christ are Man's first – a vast
anti-fugue upon the syllables
'Lama Sabachthani' cast

in twelve equal parts to symbolise
the tribes of Israel and the Serial cries
of Master Schönberg wandering the Late
Romantic wilderness. I integrate
styles from Josquin, Ritter, Metz and Fries
to middle Boulez. There are eight

young Peters who must suffer for my art,
hating Czerny's 'School' as much by heart
as me by sight. Two 'Peteresses' tease:
while one caresses individual keys
and wants, she says, to let her fingers part
across an octave-stretch with ease,

the other giggles. 'Syncopation', 'touch',
'a fugal entry', 'not so fast', 'too much
for the desired effect' – whatever, they'll guess
some double-meaning. Their sudden gentleness
can almost break my heart. After such
a lesson I cannot work unless –

But who feigns interest in what I mean
unless my sufferings can intervene?
Sometimes I'll talk to strangers, get drunk and play
ragtime in unfamiliar bars. I'll stay
until the very end unless I've been
thrown out. I'll wander drunkenly

defying the empty streets to demonstrate
affection. The falling rain will delegate
for all creation. Enough! Peter's gone
already, and the piano lid's slammed down.
Scarf, coat, hat. The empty plate,
the cup and spoon returned. Upon

the table a folded five-pound note I know
is mine. I take it and her thanks, then go
quickly from the house. At Peter's cry
I turn to see a snowman almost high
enough for Schubert. My oratorio
awaits, however – and so I wave goodbye.

THE GODS THAT I KNOW BEST

When you turned away I felt their depth and distance
meet in me as five delicate
senses; they coloured-in their eyes
and their divinity.

They named all men, all animals and things;
all their anxieties, their tenderness
and joy – and all in silence. They proved
their arguments for love

by metaphor. You'd turned your face to one side
and wouldn't speak. You stared at the electric-
light. Though your eyes were watering
and hurt, nothing was said

as you gathered my clamouring senses into a kiss.
If only the gods that I know best could thus
stammer-out their needs
and affirmations. Instead

they wrench these depths and distances apart to pierce
me through – to prove the furthest moments
of my life are closer now
than you could ever be.

THESE DAYS

Those I exiled long ago for heresies
excusing death have now returned.
And with a dignified despair they praise
the nonsense I have learned
to wonder at. Their subtleties
soon scorn what precious fears remain:
they argue my divine election;
flatter all my dismal dreams
then crown me, emperor. It seems
that I have absolute command
of oceans, mountains and the skies;
the laws of chance, like sand,
drift as I will – my sovereignty's
complete.

Those I exiled long ago have grown discreet
with their advice. These days they are concerned
with only what might best amuse – what treat
might stimulate or soothe their lord. Warned,
the court considers in poor taste
laborious pleasures based
on finding different ways to prove
the hour-hand does, or does not move,
they've laid philosophy aside
to show me how to raise the dead.
   Instead I sense my empire as the echo
of its dying emperor – as though
both time and space are being forced apart
by clumsy shadows tearing at my heart.

INHERITANCE

Although there are nettles here, and thorns,
you will not be stung. Trust me. I've something
to show you made from twigs, bird-spittle, down
and journeyings in all weathers.
See how easily your hand covers
the nest and its eggs. How weightless they are.
Your fingernail, so very much smaller than mine,
can trace the delicate shell's blue veins
until they crack apart, letting silence
spill into your hand. There is a sense
of separation almost too great to bear
– and suddenly you long to crush all colour
from these pale blue eggs, for in their brief
fragility you recognise as grief
the overwhelming tenderness you feel.
This is your inheritance:
your fist clenched on yolk and broken shell,
on fragments of an unfamiliar tense.

CLAIMING MY INHERITANCE

I paused, then briefly tried to clear the mess
of yolk-slime and albumen. My distress
was private: I could not explain
what made me run home faster than
I ever ran before.

                Since then I've taken pains
to learn the language of what's done and said
(in restaurants, in stations, on the beach, in bed)
to friends (observing gender, number, business/social),
my fellow-guests and God. For interpersonal
dynamics read *non-verbal empathy*: offence
or reinforcement at a glance. I'm quick to sense
unhappiness in others – that reassuring smile
(too well-timed), that altered tone of voice. My skill
at recognising joy is rather minimal,
however – seeming to suggest
the world is one vast Rorschach test.
I've learnt the words for things and feelings: how and when
to use them. In making conversation,
love and enemies I take especial care
no accent-lapse, no unfamiliar
tense construction, clumsy phrase
or hesitation (worst of all) betrays
I am a foreigner.

After I had crushed the eggs. A pause:

as if the colours of the earth and sky –

as if all laws affirming spontaneity –

As if the present tense were happening too soon
the fence I stood beside became a wooden thing,
the gate was iron-lengths – heated, hammered, bent
and riveted in place years earlier. I leant
against it. I struck it, but could not animate the dead
place to suffer for me. Instead,
the emptiness that stained
the empty sky above me blue,
gave definition to
my isolation.
Only this completed world remained.

The older I become the more
I am aware of exile, of longing for –

I clench my fist on nothing and hold on.

THE COLOUR OF MY MOTHER'S EYES

When I was eight years old I lived in a province
where Charlemagne's slightest wish was law;
and the woman I might have been
he made his empress.

For twelve hundred years we held court
among the dead men and the mad men:
seated side by side we stroked
any stray cat that came demanding power
– and to make the fighting cocks scream
how I'd clap and clap my beautiful hands!

He was overthrown one midsummer's day
– and as the rivers, woodlands, meadows and stonework
of the empire rushed into me, sunlight
crackled in my discarded clothes.

So do not ask me the colour of my mother's eyes:
for nowadays all I know for certain is
that while the exiled Charlemagne walks to and fro,
his courtiers amuse themselves with electricity
making the dead jerk and the living scream
with laughter.

MY GRANDFATHER DREAMS TWICE OF FLANDERS

My grandfather dreamt he was trying hard to die
and no one would help him.
He dreamt he went walking across Flanders field,
and he saw the companies of dead men
whose screaming he still hears night after night.

The countryside was a woman dressed in red.
He saw her courted briefly by a million men
carrying bayonets and mortars; her face
turning towards his, turned his to stone
and made the white clouds whirl dizzily overhead.

My grandfather dreamt that he was six years old
and a woman decked in flowers or blood
was guiding him to Flanders field:

he saw ungathered poppies scattered on the floor
and the ceiling tilting crazily
and the lights swaying;
shadows tumbling out of the darkness
beckoned him everywhere.

He saw her heaping flowers into a bed.
Then one by one she took the shadows
to lie with her, and one
by one he saw them disappear.

POEM FOR MY FATHER

A flame shivers within me
and by its light I see hills and forests and cities,
the rest is darkness.

I haunt myself since childhood
since when that solitary flame has cast each moment's shadow
as the heart's beat forces the moment on.

After he died my father performed miracles.
He walks before me with his eyes closed
guiding me to other hills, other forests and cities
where I haunt those who live there.

Time and again his dead hand reaches for mine,
then I forget the laws of love and territory
and pass as helplessly through stone as through air
where he follows after, obliterating my path.

Seen by this trembling flame, the years are in disorder.
My father became confused by so many shadows
circling the sky

that now he sees through my eyes:
seeking a world without light and without darkness,
and to guide me there.

MY INHERITANCE

We've spent all afternoon in bed, hardly speaking:
Outside, a bird is just about to sing; listen:

   Since my father's death I've managed to disgrace
a dozen hearts and beds, making each a court
where I might love and talk of love, yet still support
whatever sinecures most pleasantly debase
that love into allegiance. Courtly etiquette
could make my servitude appear as *politesse*
– well-practised passion, warmth. I needed nakedness
to show my feelings, even to myself – to let
myself go. I parodied ingratiating
courtly roles: the tyrant seen deliberating
with cruel disinterest; the diplomat who's paid
to kiss away the pain; the fool who tumbles up
and down the stairs for some applause and won't believe
he's ever hurt, the show goes on because he'll stop
at nothing for a laugh. He's dangerous, mad:
needing an audience he's never last to leave.

   My father's relatives were introduced to me:
they shook my hand and asked how I was getting on.
An aunt from Perth had made us sandwiches and tea;
her husband, talking of his crops, remarked that rain
would be the death of him. I laughed aloud but he
refused to see the joke. The relatives were shocked.
   Earlier my father's corpse had been conveyed
from sight and burned. A shaky plastic screen had blocked
the view while Bach, beginning in mid-fugue, was played
to ease us through our grief. Afterwards we prayed
briefly; then Bach was pressed upon to serve once more
– a half-toccata saw us almost to the door.

Sorrow, deep regret, ten minutes' mourning-muzak,
silences and sympathy on double-time
plus tips. Electric motors jerked him quickly back
to an eternity whose span, with pantomime
precision, began just where a black-trimmed velveteen
conveyor-belt ran out. Everything had been
well-organised and went like clockwork, we looked on.
The lodger drove us home.
                                    Ten years ago today
my life began by launching father down that slipway
to unsounded oceans' measureless mirage.
Champagne against the coffin-sides! Bon Voyage!
Call up unearthly winds to speed his odyssey
among the kingdoms of the dead. An embarkation
service said in Greek to keep the Classic tone.
I slaughtered bulls, burnt thigh-bones wrapped in fat, the slow
uncoiling smoke I read for signs while letting flow
my filial tears unchecked etc. 'Take care
– to leave the rest to me!' I cried as son and heir.

Since then whatever I might wish to do
seems scarcely mine, but is at once anticipated
by a sense of his return: ten years seen through
this one imaginary moment delegated
to describe mortality. In time the ghosts
and demons we create as though from nothing, to share
our loneliness, become our overlords. These hosts
of our invisibility demand our blood
to let them speak. My father's spirit cries aloud,
claiming back the life he gave me – and I, his creature,
cling even to my despair.

All my subtle thoughts have led
only to subtler thoughts. Like Penelope,
forced to stay behind, I weave each hated thread
into its rightful place then tear the tapestry

apart, dreaming I cancel-out my grief. Instead,
some stars have been displaced, some distant oceans spread
elsewhere and then denied. Alone, I celebrate
both love and loss of love together in one image
of desperation. Dream-suitors come to me. They state
conditions for my next imaginary marriage:
they strip the gardens, fields and cellars; they desecrate
the family shrines; they force me to adjudicate
their drunken games. When seasons meet in me as darkness
– then hatred and desire are all I need to bless
my dream-adulteries.

                              If I would live
then I must suffer everything I am. The dead
are not responsible for me – they cannot give
a little meaning to my life. I have paid
for my inheritance with all I have – the price
is fixed at that, and I must settle for nothing less
if I would live and be myself. I am afraid
to bargain with the dead, but must do. The emptiness
between what is, what might have been, is their domain.
I must journey there alone, or else remain
pretending to reason with the mad – their dreams betray
this world's a metaphor quite suddenly come true
and incorruptible, as Time foreshortens to
a gesture of ambiguous delay.

   When you and I make love we enter silence:
the noise of kings, courtiers and fools
does not reach us here. Sincerity, pretence
and tact lose meaning; established courtly rules
are valueless. We kiss and kiss again, as though
caresses have so weighted down Time we know
whatever is – is ours; and every tense
becomes a plaything we can share.
   Listen, a bird is singing at our bedroom window:
its song is all the world – and trapped out there.